It's Okay to Not be Okay!

Poems Through Healing

Rasheeda Frazier

Copyright © 2022 by Rasheeda Frazier

All rights reserved. No part of this publication may be reproduced, distributed, or transmitted in any form or by any means, including photocopying, recording, or other electronic or mechanical methods, without the prior written permission of the publisher, except in the case of brief quotations embodied in critical reviews and certain other noncommercial uses permitted by copyright law. For permission requests, write to the author, addressed "Attention: Permissions " at
rasheeda.frazier1@gmail.com

Frazier Publication

Print ISBN: 979-8-218-04304-9

Printed in the United States of America on SFI Certified paper.

I dedicate this book to those who stood by my side during this journey and most importantly through my healing. I also dedicate this book to my aunt Emma Jean Powell. You are missed!

Rest in peace!

Just when you thought someone didn't think or feel like you did, you stumbled upon this book!

Contents

Butterflies	8
Escape	10
Grace	16
Running	18
It is what you make it	21
Words	24
Change	27
Crown	29
Dream	31
Goodbye	32
Flatline	35
Inner Child	37
Money	41
Trip	43
Numb	45
Paper	47
Reasons	49
I AM	51
The Unknown	54
Caged	57
Love	60
Prayer	62
About the Author	67

Butterflies

I use to get butterflies for the guys that couldn't look me in the eyes and say, I don't want you, but prize that lies below the skies.
I'd deny my emotions just to hit that love potion.
The wanting to just be wanted.
Past trauma that hadn't been confronted.
Being me for him, while he was doing him for them.
I was never in his vision and yet, he got me with such precision.
But if pain has taught me anything, feelings are never facts.
And how I want my heart to be loved is my decision.

"You are enough!"

Escape

How did we get here and how do we leave?
Looking for the quickest exit out my head.
I've found the comfiest place to sleep which is my bed.
Closing my eyes and poof, a new destination.
The cheapest flight to anywhere but here.
Leaving my body to find my soul.
Gliding through the air as I look below.
A bird?
A plane?
Oh the bird.
So free and heard.
By everyone around them, before the whole world is fully awake, you know you can count on the songs of the wild.
To wake up, care free.
The once happy child.
The reality is that reality isn't real but a made up idea of how life should be.

"There is power in not always being right"

Cell- Sexual

I want you to make love to my mind, as I divulge what I've been thinking.
How I articulate my emotions.
See my words as you hear what I am speaking.
To understand this machine, you need to turn on your ears, and switch how you think, just to get me.
Even just for a minute.
I want you to love my brain as it is the most powerful thing on me.
Built custom from my childhood story.
The mountain that stands before me,
Is my thoughts and worries.
So I climb them.
I want you to fall in love with the way I process.
My mind is beautifully challenging.

Sparks of neurons storing the memories of the past and as time goes on those memories are replaced with the last.

Cognitive dissertation, word for word, letter for letter.

Thought provoking, as the lights turn on and you finally get it.

I want you to hold dear the understanding that my minds forever altered by the trauma of my past and yet here I am slowly freeing myself.

Free at last.

I want you to love my brain and every query.

As this is my powerhouse that holds my story!

"You are not your past trauma"

Grace

I'm in a weird space with life, trying to understand my place and give room to allow love and grace in my mind so my heart can feel fine. Healing the soul, so my body feels full and together the temple is praised with reward and this person can move forward in the life they don't understand.

In the world they didn't ask to be in.

Finally, trying to swim and break the chains that keep me under.

Suffocating on the pain and anger.

Drowned by the insanity that lives inside my brain It keeps me wondering.

When does my life begin?

Is everything I do a sin?

Is this hell on earth and heaven within?

"There is value in not always being right"

Running

Growing up, I've always dreamed of running far away.
Then once I was able to, nothing could stand in my way.
With the slightest hint of fear, my feet were nowhere near.
They left to another place to start over, where they felt they had peace.
Only to be planted in more hurt and disbelief.
I've walked 10,000 moons inside my own shoes.
No man or woman can take me back to that place.
I'll walk 10,000 more just to be the best me.
Not running because it got hard or because someone stabbed me yet again, straight through my heart.
I'll run to the end because I pray the end will be great.

I'll run because I want to reach the finish line.

I'll run for good reasons.

With pain comes a healing season.

We just have to hang in there and fight, instead of flight.

Stand, instead of run.

"Your value is internal"

It is what you make it

I was asked: Does the pain create the music or does the music prompt the words that create?
Like if I could be happy and still write.
Or does creativity come with pain?
So, I sit here again writing off the brain.
Thinking of my future and the work I have put in.
Being aware of my words and going to sleep to affirmations.
The more I see the positive, the closer I see a confirmation.
Destination 2 blocks around the corner.
Walk, run, ride, or drive.
I don't want to do either, I want to fly:
Over my my dreams and into my passions.
Full force into my blessings.
No longer stuck, I keep progressing.

Continuing the mental healing, one day with every session.
Music can help depression and music can be a blessing.
Take it for what it is or go and make your own message.
Positive, no pain, and yet my hand could still write just what I hear in my brain.
So if it's sad, it's sad.
But if you create it with the mind to be elated, then anything you come up with will be upgraded.

"Cry if you need to"

Words

Sometimes, I feel like I should be doing more.
Making a difference in my own world,
Or maybe it's the feeling of being bored.
The everyday struggle of being in the present,
And the want for instant gratification,
just to get a temporary satisfaction,
of being happy even for a moment.
The next move is far away, but it's the path to it that matters.
The understanding that you have to enjoy the process, not just the outcome.
The will to understand that which can't be understood.
The knowledge to know that just because they do, doesn't mean you should.
The burst of motivation because you subconsciously see the future.
Speak words into existence.

For everything you want should come with hard work and persistences.

"I will give myself grace when I make mistakes"

Change

Sometimes, I am afraid of the change that hasn't come, but is waiting in the foreground.
The thought of being more than you could ever imagine.
To step up is to step away from the life you once revolved in.
To sit in your own feelings, meant you fought to get some healing.
The feeling to just get up and run.
Anxiety: the death that never comes.
People's words they stabbed like daggers.
My brain became polluted.
How did life get so diluted?
To thinking that it's normal for how you were raised.
Abuse then becomes praised
because "that's just the black families' way."

"I Am Worth it"

Crown

I had a lot of male men, but none have yet to deliver.
So, I sit with my plate full and wait to just give a sliver.
When you have yourself a lineup, but only one you give your time up.
Delete the whole entire team and post a whole new sign-up.
Accessing the situation and peeping the conversation.
These men don't want anything, but time in your deepest secret.
A private eye into the meeting they knew they weren't supposed to be in.
Be smart, wear your crown and no matter who you're around: be you and only you. Girl keep walking and don't dare turn around, because if he knew what I knew; Then he wouldn't mess around.

I love myself because who'll love me if I
knock off my crown every time a man denies me
or doesn't keep me around.
I love me to walk away.
That's how it should always be, if he turns the
other cheek then baby that's just a blessing.
Pray for yourself that you are ready for when
the perfect one steps in.
I'm a girl of many talents, I make words turn
into ballots.

"Perfection is a myth not reality"

Dream

Dreams far and past, I thought that everything that came good would always last.
We the people afraid of what's before us, even more stuck deep in what will destroy us.
The mind is only as strong as the heart.
So, take up your worst fear and tear it apart.
Sitting in silence feelings, going wild.
Anxiety on high while my heart is on fire.
Feeling young, wild and free is one of my many desires.
Love me and you?
If I can't love me then why should you?
Hurt people, hurt people: It's just evil for evil.
I'm in my healing season.
Not everything lasts forever.
It's either a lesson or it's a blessing!

Goodbye

I was right to say goodbye because later became forever.
When you want to run, but you can't because your feet are bandaged.
When you want to speak, but it's best that you keep your feelings to yourself.
When you want to scream, but that'd be too loud. Best to not disturb your neighbor.
When you want to cry, but the sun won't let the dark clouds cover.
And when you want to die, but your own hands know that if they hold each other tight, punch air and fight the fight; then maybe life will be much clearer.

"Flaws are not signs of being inadequate"

Flatline

We live on earth just trying to find our meaning.
I feel like my body isn't mine for many reasons.
My heart does beat and I can feel the feelings.
The ones I want and then the ones I needed.
How can one breathe if they feel so defeated?
It feels like the world is cascading through my ribs, puncturing the only thing keeping me here.
HEAR, every vein burst into tears as the muscles rip the love, the pain, the joy and the anger from the person I have become.
No more means that we are done.
Mind radio silent.
Flatline until I'm cold to the touch.
I was born into a world that doesn't like me.
Can't remember life before 5 because I was tiny.
Both parents were broken so they unintentionally hurt me.

Then a man walks into my life, destroys my mind and now I have to find me!

How much pain?

And at what cost?

My only hope is that I regain life.

A spike from flatline to, " I believe we have a pulse."

Looking around me I can see that half the world is lost.

Searching for answers in people we barely trust.

But self-healing and therapy is a must.

"Mistakes are growth opportunities"

Inner Child

I miss the days I don't remember...
I miss the kid that knew no fear.
I miss the kid that had so much laughter.
I miss the heart that was filled with love.
I miss the endless days of life.
I miss the days before I knew how life really was.
I miss the girl who didn't care about how she looked.
I miss the days I could speak in front of people and not be afraid.
Honestly, I miss the old me that I can't even remember.
Needless to say, we were all fearless.
Then life came around, knocked us down, and caged our inner child.
So, as an adult, I say this:
I wish I didn't let them hurt you.
I wish I could have protected you.

I wish I could have told you everything will be alright!
I wish I could hold you through your sleepless nights.
So, greetings from the older you, we got this and we still have work to do.
For now, I'll have to be the mother we wished we could have seen and one day we can be set free of all the pain that was brought on us.
My then, now and forever.
I'm a girl of many talents, I make words turn into ballots.

"Feelings are not facts"

Money

They say money can't buy happiness, know that is a lie.
In today's society, without it, we will die.
To eat what's right means sleepless nights.
To be healthy means self-medication and google symptom checking.
To some, it may just come a blessing.
For others they have to work
Til' skin turns to callus and bone then become fragile.
The rich still hold the power,
while everyone else gets devoured;
In debt, and things we try to manage.
Recession has caused a panic.

*"Lord grant me the serenity to accept the things I can not change...
The courage to change the things I can...
And the wisdom to know the difference!"*

Trip

As I close my eyes, I'm greeted by the beautiful colors I've never experienced.

The shapes and patterns that dance and change quickly.

Then to open them and see that I am now underwater.

Floating below, watching as the surface above moves slowly.

The bright blue skies have sprinkles of green, the stars are shingling bright colors.

It's beautifully challenging to take it all in, to feel at peace with yourself and the world you created!

Because you are in control of your mind as you travel deep within your soul, searching for the child in you that was let down.

*"I choose to enjoy the process,
not just the outcome"*

Numb

Becoming numb to life and the things within.
The first heartbreak hurts, but the ones thereafter dig deeper.
You cry no tears, but you feel the bandage being ripped off and the holes dug deeper.
The pain of not knowing why you feel hurt.
But the urge to hold back tears because you're better than that which holds your fears and pockets your emotions.
Too much pain and you become hopeless.
You become an empty vessel.
Numb to the feelings of being loved.
Afraid to be you because each time you are who you are, they walk out and you're left with a scar.
I'm just the girl that FELL and you didn't CATCH, but it's okay, I got back UP brushed

myself off and knew to NEVER trip over you again!

But I'm still numb!

"Anxiety is a down payment on something that didn't happen"

Paper

How can you still hear thoughts when the only thought you actually hear is the words coming off the wood pulp that you hold in your hand?
As you read, it doesn't process, you forget just what you processed.
I didn't hear my subconscious because I was occupied with what my eyes see.
The black lines spaced out to give thought to the mind as letters A through Z bounce across the paper.

"Everyone makes mistakes, including me"

Reasons

They say things happen for a reason!
And things happen because there is a better plan ahead.
But why did I have to spare my heart and soul?
I feel so empty inside.
I just want to be happy.
One minute I'm okay, and one minute something different.
Like I am not here and the tears that run down my mountain flow heavy.
Tears drop for any and no reason.

"I will give myself grace"

I AM

I see what they see when they see me.
For a long time, I didn't even want to be me because if I know who I am then no one can tell me, for I know…

I am beautiful…
At my worst, and even more at my best
I am smart…
Even when I have a moment and it becomes questionable.
I am creative.
I am funny…
Even if you don't think I am.
I am caring.
I am loyal.
I am supportive.
I am adventurous.
I am a vibe.

I am strong…

Even when I don't want to be.

I am a survivor.

I am ambitious.

I am determined.

I am kind…

Even when others aren't kind to me.

I am successful.

I am healing.

I am amazing.

I am blessed.

I am an artist.

"Yesterday has passed, tomorrow is not promised, So, live in the moment!"

The Unknown

Sometimes, I feel like drifting away.
Into the sunrise far away from the pain.
This can't be my forever and most certainly not my today!
Feeling as if you have to be alone while you fix your pain.
Knowing you're strong and you've put in the work and also knowing that healing is forever.
So, is the work really done?
Should you stay alone?
Hoping that the person you share your world with can handle the person you are and be ready for the person you will become.
Wanting to run but you're trying to plant and propagate your soles into the soul of the earth and grow as tall as the Hyperion tree.
Go as deep at the ocean breathes,
But I'm afraid of that water,

Or more-so what's underneath,

What lies below.

The creatures of the unknown.

The unknown..

"My past trauma doesn't control my future"

Caged

Blank pages.

Empty spaces.

Open cages.

Arms reaching out barely touching what's in hindsight.

Day turns into night.

Maybes turn into mights.

Same thing but I just might.

Maybe try again tomorrow.

If tomorrow is given.

Because today, I barely made it.

Just existing.

Hardly listening.

Stop resisting.

The urge to run from your fears

And fight them.

Voice quiet.

Mind silent.

Soul's a riot.

Looking for my body

Because, well, they are separate searching for

each other.

Pages filled.

Spaces occupied.

Cage is still open.

"It's okay to ask for help"

Love

I've never known a healthy love, by anyone I've been with or even my parents.
I barely know it for myself and still I learn.
I yearn for the love that can heal a heart.
The pain from the beginning and the healing at the start.
I wish holding your breath didn't mean dying inside and being hopeful didn't come at the cost of getting hurt.
That love actually had a meaning and work was paid not based on worth.
I want my cup to run over, filled with the things that feed my mind, body and soul, so I can fill your cup with the things that you need.

"Positivity starts in your mind"

Prayer

Now, I lay me down to sleep.
I pray dear Lord, please keep my mind at peace.
And if these fears they get the best of me,
I pray I fight and keep serenity.
Please heal these wounds, I did not self-inflict.
Got all this pain that I've been dealing with.
Can't close my eyes without the images.
Of how life was and wasn't spent.
There'I cry because I feel the beatings,
Of many years of being lost and treated,
as if I had a heart with out no feelings.
Reach to the sky, but always hit the ceiling.
I pray for those who don't believe that love,
can heal the pain in the amygdala.
Feed off the energy of those around me.
So, keep the negative far behind me.
We came a long way from where we started.
'We' as in me, my soul, and the thoughts that deride me.

One day, my mind won't wonder what's life?
And why even bother.
What if he and leaves?
Do I care to even see tomorrow?
Trying to stay sane and let go of all the sorrow.
Remember the good and know the pain is borrowed from past experiences; we soon will conquer.
Paid in full, I have no space to be bothered.
Break all the behaviors of past hurt encounters.
Know you're a queen and need to trust the process.
Though it may seem that you are lost and you keep going through nonsense.
Things will get better.
Life will come full circle.
Part of my soul feels it's a lie I practice in rehearsal.
Don't care, don't cry, telling myself it's okay!
You will be loved by not just yourself but someone special one day.

"Life can be beautiful. You just have to keep going and find it"

Stage one of my healing....

Many more to come!!

About the Author

Photographer: Rasheeda Frazier

I was born and raised in Canton, Ohio and have since moved trying to find myself. Through my adult journey of healing, I gained a new realization about life and what I am interested in. Who would have known I'd be a photographer, business owner, poet and author. Even though life has rained on my parade several times, I found that writing was an outlet to express the feelings in my head that I could not speak.

www.ingramcontent.com/pod-product-compliance
Lightning Source LLC
Chambersburg PA
CBHW070209100426
42743CB00013B/3114